COCKROACHES

NICOLE HELGET

Published by Creative Education

P.O. Box 227, Mankato, Minnesota 56002

Creative Education is an imprint of The Creative Company

Design and production by Stephanie Blumenthal

Printed in the United States of America

Photographs by Alamy Images (Eureka, FLPA, Holt Studios International Ltd,
James Caldwell), James Castner

Library of Congress Cataloging-in-Publication Data

Helget, Nicole Lea, 1976–
Cockroaches / by Nicole Helget.
p. cm. — (BugBooks)
Includes index.
ISBN-13: 978-1-58341-540-5
1. Cockroaches—Juvenile literature. I. Title.

QL505.5.H45 2007
595.7'28—DC22   2006018237

First Edition
2 4 6 8 9 7 5 3 1

THE SUN HAS SET.

THE HOUSE IS DARK. HUNDREDS OF FEET TAP ACROSS THE FLOOR. THEY MARCH UNDER THE STOVE. THEY CLIMB ON THE TOASTER. COCKROACHES HAVE INVADED THE KITCHEN!

COCKROACHES ARE INSECTS.
MOST COCKROACHES ARE BROWN

OR BLACK. THEY

CAN BE AS SMALL

AS A DIME OR AS

BIG AS AN EGG.

COCKROACHES CAN RUN FAST.
THEY CAN SWIM AND FLY, TOO.

Most cockroaches are a dark color.

HEADLESS ROACHES   A cockroach's brain is spread through its whole body. A cockroach without a head can live for a week! It finally dies because it cannot eat or drink anything.

A COCKROACH'S EYES CAN SEE IN ALL DIRECTIONS. COCKROACHES HAVE FEELERS CALLED ANTENNAE (AN-*TEN*-NAY) ON THEIR HEADS. THE FEELERS ARE USED TO SMELL, TOUCH, AND TASTE.

Cockroaches' antennae can be very long.

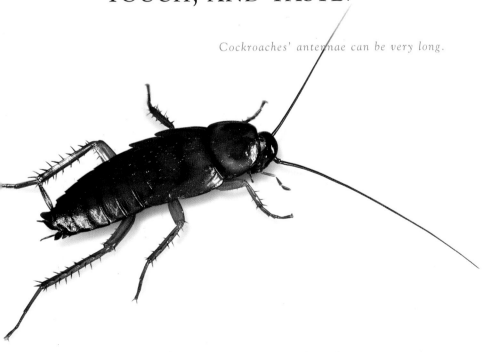

COCKROACHES HAVE FOUR WINGS AND SIX LEGS. COCKROACHES DO NOT USE THEIR WINGS TO FLY VERY OFTEN. THEY USUALLY RUN AWAY FROM DANGER. COCKROACH LEGS ARE LONG AND THIN. THEY HELP THE COCKROACH RUN FAST.

Cockroaches have small heads and long bodies.

A cockroach's belly is hard.

THE BIGGEST PART OF A COCK-ROACH IS ITS BELLY. THE BELLY IS HARD AND IS COVERED BY WINGS. THEY PROTECT THE COCKROACH LIKE A SHIELD. THE BELLY ALSO HAS TINY AIR HOLES. THEY LET THE COCKROACH BREATHE.

A COCKROACH BEGINS ITS LIFE IN AN EGG SAC. WHEN COCKROACH

BABIES ARE READY TO HATCH, THE EGG SAC SPLITS OPEN. LOTS OF BABY COCK-ROACHES CRAWL OUT OF THE EGGS.

Female cockroaches make egg sacs.

A BABY COCKROACH IS CALLED A "NYMPH" (*NIMF*). IT LIKES TO EAT GARBAGE AND OLD FOOD. A NYMPH EATS SO MUCH THAT IT HAS TO SHED ITS  SKIN. AFTER A WHILE, THE NYMPH STOPS GROW- ING. THE NYMPH BECOMES AN ADULT COCKROACH.

A nymph's skin turns from light to dark.

GOOD SWIMMERS Cockroaches can hold their breath for 15 minutes. They sometimes get into houses by swimming up drain pipes. Then they crawl out of the pipes and into sinks and bathtubs.

COCKROACHES LIKE WARM, DAMP PLACES. COCKROACHES LIKE TO EAT AND DRINK. THEY LIKE TO LIVE NEAR PEOPLE. PEOPLE HAVE LOTS OF FOOD AND WATER IN THEIR HOUSES.

Cockroaches are always looking for crumbs.

PEOPLE DO NOT LIKE TO HAVE
COCKROACHES IN THEIR HOUSES.

COCKROACHES CAN SPREAD DISEASE.
THEY LEAVE BAD SMELLS, TOO. IT IS
HARD TO GET RID OF COCKROACHES.

Cockroaches like to hide in cracks.

HISSING COCKROACH *Some people keep the hissing cock-roach as a pet. This big cockroach grows about three inches (7.5 cm) long. It makes a noise like a snake when it feels afraid.*

FAST RUNNERS Cockroaches are fast. They run away from predators such as birds and other bugs. They can run three miles (4.8 km) per hour. That is why it is hard to stomp on them or catch them.

SOMETIMES, PEOPLE WHO TRAVEL BRING NEW KINDS OF COCKROACHES TO NEW PLACES. COCKROACHES ARE GOOD AT FINDING NEW PLACES TO RUN AND EAT!

Most people think of cockroaches as pests.

GLOSSARY

DISEASE — A KIND OF SICKNESS

EGG SAC — A POUCH THAT A MOTHER COCKROACH PUTS ITS

        EGGS IN

INSECTS — BUGS THAT HAVE SIX LEGS

PREDATORS — ANIMALS THAT KILL AND EAT OTHER ANIMALS

SHED — TO LOSE SKIN

INDEX